SERVICE LEARNING

Volunteering for a Political Campaign

Sheila Klee

HIGH
interest
books

Children's Press
A Division of Grolier Publishing
New York / London / Hong Kong / Sydney
Danbury, Connecticut

Contributing Editor: Rob Kirkpatrick
Book Design: Michael DeLisio

Photo Credits: Cover, p. 6, 9. 14, 16, 24, 28, 31, 32, 35 by Maura
Boruchow; p. 4, 10, © AP/Wide World Photos; p. 13, 38 © International
Stock; p. 18, 20, 23, © Indexstock; p. 26, © AFP/Corbis; p. 36 © Mitchell
Gerber/Corbis; p. 41 © Joseph Sohm; ChromoSohm Inc./Corbis

Visit Children's Press on the Internet at:
http://publishing.grolier.com

Library of Congress Cataloging-in-Publication Data

Klee, Sheila.
   Volunteering for a political campaign / by Sheila Klee.
      p. cm. – (Service Learning)
   Includes bibliographical references and index.
   ISBN 0-516-23398-X (lib. bdg.) – ISBN 0-516-23576-1 (pbk.)
   1. Youth—United States—Political Activity--Juvenile literature. 2. Political
participation—United States—Juvenile literature. 3. Electioneering—United
States—Juvenile literature. [1. Political participation. 2. Politics, Practical.
   3. Elections.]
   I. Title. II. Series.

HQ799.2.P6 K583 2000
323.7'2—dc21
                                                              00-028266

CONTENTS

INTRODUCTION

American flags snap in the wind. They form the background to smiling faces on billboards. Posters sprout up on lawns around the neighborhood. Bright new bumper stickers appear on cars. A sea of red, white, and blue surrounds you. Sound familiar? It's political campaign season again.

Behind the images is a chance at power. The winning candidate will have the power to help make laws about important issues. He or she might make decisions that will affect the environment and programs for health, transportation, and education.

Candidates depend on campaign workers. These workers spread a candidate's

Political campaigns are a big part of American life.

*Many campaign workers
are service-learning volunteers.*

message and help the candidate to win votes. Some campaign workers are paid. Many others are volunteers. They work for a campaign because they believe in it. They believe that helping a particular candidate to win an election is the first step in helping to change something about which they care. That's where you come into the picture.

CHAPTER ONE

WHAT IS SERVICE LEARNING?

Both community service and service learning use volunteer (unpaid) workers to help in the community. But service learning is something more, too. That's the "learning" part. Volunteer work can turn into a service-learning project. A service-learning project helps you to learn something about yourself and your community. It also helps you to learn new skills, such as how to write a letter to a public official. You may even improve the skills you already have.

THE GROWTH OF SERVICE LEARNING

The idea of combining community service with learning grew throughout the 1980s and

1990s. Young people began groups on their own. Groups such as these were called grassroots groups. In grassroots groups such as COOL2Serve, students ran their own service-learning projects.

The U.S. government also helped service learning to catch on. Two presidents, George Bush and Bill Clinton, have supported service-learning activities. Now, in the twenty-first century, the service-learning movement is larger than ever before. High schools, colleges, and community organizations throughout the country run service-learning programs.

The National and Community Service Trust Act

The National and Community Service Trust Act of 1993 is a federal (from the national government) law that supports service learning. This law defines service-learning programs as programs that:

Talk to your guidance counselor about service-learning opportunities at your school.

- help students learn and develop
- help others in a way they need
- help you become a good citizen
- are part of your schoolwork or other educational program
- provide time for you to reflect on your experience

SPONSORS

Many organizations try to serve the public without making a profit. They are called nonprofit organizations. Nonprofit organizations such as 4H, Earth Force, and the Close Up

Volunteers can help inform voters about candidates.

Foundation sponsor service-learning programs in schools and community organizations. Government agencies, such as the Corporation for National Service, sponsor them also. See the back of this book for details on how to contact these groups.

WHERE DOES POLITICAL CAMPAIGNING FIT IN?

It's easy to see how some service-learning projects help people. Some organizations set up recycling centers. Others fix up local playgrounds. Some help the elderly or the disabled get to the doctor or the supermarket. But how do you help your community by working on a political campaign? Doesn't political work just help the candidate and his or her supporters?

Making the System Work

By working on a campaign, you take part in a political system. One way to serve your town, county, state, or nation is to help choose its leaders. You may not be old enough to vote. Yet you still can be an active member of society. One way to do this is by volunteering to work on a campaign. By doing so, you become part of an important process. You help to make sure people know more about a candidate so that they can make more informed choices when voting.

WE THE PEOPLE

The government of the United States is called a representative democracy. In this form of government, people elect officials to represent them. We elect officials by voting for them. When you vote, you help to choose your government leaders.

Close Up Foundation

The Close Up Foundation believes that "Democracy is not a spectator sport." This saying means that people should not just sit back and let other people do all the work. To have an effective democracy, everyone should use his or her right to vote.

The Close Up Foundation seeks to teach people about the importance of voting. The foundation runs programs on the local, state, and national level for both students and teachers.

COMBINING CAMPAIGN WORK AND SCHOOLWORK

Some schools require students to do service learning before they can graduate. If your

*Ask your teacher if you can do a campaign
project as part of your schoolwork.*

school does not require service learning, ask
your teacher about planning a service-
learning project. Working on a political
campaign gives you many opportunities. You
can combine your campaign work with a
class at school. For example, you could study
voting results for math class. You could
research government laws for civics class or
social studies class. You could study political

Campaign work can help you to develop organizational and communication skills.

trends for history class. Figure out what interests you most about campaigning. Then tell your teacher about it.

WHAT YOU CAN LEARN

You can learn new job skills when you work on a political campaign. You also can improve the skills you already have. For example, suppose you want your candidates to meet with the public. First you will need to find a building that you can use for a meeting space. You might have to make a few phone calls to places around town. You will need to explain why you need the building. Working on a project such as this will build your communication skills.

You also will need to advertise the event. Are you good at drawing or lettering? You could make posters and flyers to tell people about the event. Are you good at writing? You could write a statement to send to radio stations and

DID YOU KNOW?

A press release should be no more than one page long, and it should include the name and phone number of the person whom people can call for information. Your press release should say whose project it is, what the project is, when and where it will take place, and why you're doing it.

newspapers so that they can cover the event. This kind of statement is called a press release.

*You might be able to find information
about political candidates on the Internet.*

Successfully planning an event shows that
you have organizational skills and communication skills. It also shows that you can stick
with a task until it is finished. All of these
are great things to list on an application for
college or a job.

Most important, you will learn about the
voting process. You will understand what it
takes for a candidate to get on the ballot (list
of the candidates for voters). You will find out

about the role money plays in a campaign. Knowing these things will help you to become a smarter and more active citizen. You will come away with a new sense of power. You will understand how you are connected to your government.

WHY SHOULD YOU GET INVOLVED?

Many people feel unconnected to their government. They believe that the government has little effect on their day-to-day lives. What do you think?

Do you ride a bus to school? Do you take one to the

FAST FACT

There are 85,006 state and local governments in the United States. There are more than half a million elected officials.

mall? Do you go to a library? Are there too many students in your classes? Are there a lot of new businesses coming to your city? Does your town have parks? Does it have a recreation program for its citizens? Does your city

Read your local newspaper to follow upcoming elections.

have a prison, or a casino? The local, state, and national governments pay for, and therefore affect, all of these things. Whether you realize it or not, government affects everyone's lives.

Not all schools allow students to work on political campaigns. You will have to ask your service-learning coordinator. Perhaps you will be allowed to choose a nonpartisan (showing no favor for any candidate) political project. Look at Chapter Three for an activity you can do for either a campaign or for a nonpartisan political project.

CHAPTER TWO

GETTING STARTED

Elections take place at different times in the year or only during particular years, depending on where you live. Find out when elections occur in your voting area. Call the national office or the nearest regional chapter of the League of Women Voters to find out if it is an election year. Or read a newspaper. Articles about upcoming elections always appear in newspapers. Once you know when an election will occur, take a close look at the issues and the candidates.

ISSUES

About which issues do you care? What is being done about them now? What do you

think should be done? Will laws about these issues be made by the national, state, or local government?

Suppose you are concerned about the environment. You could focus on a national issue, such as whether animal habitats should be protected against mining, logging, or construction. You could volunteer to help a candidate that is running for a national office. If you are concerned about keeping the local water supply clean, you might want to volunteer to help a local candidate who wants to stop industries from dumping waste into the water system.

VOTING HISTORY

Find out as much as you can about the work a candidate has done for the community. How has he or she voted on issues in the past? A lot of information you get during election time is biased (favoring a particular person). Newspapers and magazines can be biased too—especially in editorials (opinion state-

Are you concerned about the environment?
Find a candidate who feels the same way.

ments). However, you still should read as many magazines and newspapers as you can. The more information you get, the better. Read a daily newspaper. Attend debates. Listen to debates or interviews on the radio, or watch them on television. The political Web sites listed in the back of this book will lead you to a number of sources of information.

POLITICAL DISCUSSIONS

Talk to everyone you can—friends, parents, teachers, and others—about their opinions of the candidates and the issues. Listen with an open mind. Talking about your ideas will help you to form your own opinions.

A MATTER OF CHOICE

You've thought about the issues and have researched the available candidates. Now, choose the person you think will do the best job if elected. Who will try to accomplish some of your goals?

*Talking with friends, parents, or teachers
can help you to form your own opinions about politics.*

Pros and Cons

No candidate is perfect. You probably will not agree with your candidate about everything. For example, you may agree with a candidate who wants to clean up local parks. However, the same candidate may want to cut school funds to pay for park improvements. What should you do?

Find out everything that a candidate supports or does not support. You should support someone with whom you feel comfortable as your representative. You may choose a candidate who does not support everything that you support. However, if you help to elect a candidate who wants to work for some of the same goals that you have, you still will have a positive effect on your government— and your community.

POLITICAL PARTIES

Most politicians are either democrats or republicans. These groups are the two most powerful political parties in the United States. However, there are more political parties than the Democratic and Republican parties. Some other parties are the Libertarian Party, the Reform Party, the Socialist Party, and the Conservative Party.

Members of a political party tend to have similar ideas about government. However,

To which party does your candidate belong?

you cannot tell what a candidate stands for just by knowing to which party he or she belongs. For example, not all democrats stand for the same ideas. Always find out as much as you can about an individual candidate before you support him or her.

WHAT ARE YOUR POLITICS?

What are your opinions about what a government should do? Log on to the Internet and go to www.selectsmart.com. Take one of the site's political quizzes to match yourself up to a political party or a presidential candidate. This fun exercise also will help you figure out your own views. The results may surprise you. Try it with friends, too, and compare results and opinions. The quiz will lead you to the names of other political parties, rather than just the Democratic and Republican parties.

Listening to candidates debate may help you understand their stances on political issues.

CHAPTER THREE

GETTING INVOLVED

There are two more things to think about before you volunteer to work on a campaign. Think about which skills you have to offer as a campaign volunteer. Also, think about what you enjoy doing.

HOW YOU CAN HELP

Everybody has a skill to offer as a service learner. How can you help a campaign? There are many ways:

- **Information technology skills.** Are you good with computers? You can work with computers to update campaign records.
- **Communication skills.** Do you like to write? Every campaign needs people to

Every service learner can do something to support a candidate.

write letters, press releases, or speeches. Are you artistic? You could design flyers and posters for your campaign.

- **Office skills.** Are you organized? Do you enjoy talking to people? Your campaign may need you to answer phones, or send and open mail.
- **Outreach skills.** Do you like meeting new people? A candidate may ask you to give out brochures. He or she may have you make phone calls, or help set up rallies.

ACHIEVING YOUR GOALS

When you work on a campaign, you have three goals. You want to help the campaign. You want to help your community. And you want to learn something. Here are some ideas about ways to achieve your goals:

How You Help the Campaign

If you work on a candidate's campaign, your goal is to get people to vote for that candidate.

You can help a campaign by stuffing envelopes.

All of the work you do on a campaign helps get people to support your candidate. Even small tasks such as stuffing envelopes help to get out the candidate's message.

How You Help the Community
If you help a candidate to win an election, then the newly-elected official can help make positive changes. The official can help pass

*Get together and discuss your
strategies and goals for the campaign.*

laws that make your community a better place in which to live.

When you help with a political campaign, you also help your community by making people more aware of important issues. Even if your candidate doesn't win the election, the candidate's campaign still will have increased people's awareness of issues that affect them.

For example, what if your candidate wanted to help improve the garbage pickup system in your town? This kind of issue gets attention during a political campaign. Then citizens may decide to do something themselves about the garbage pickup system. When people see a campaign that involves hard-working volunteers, they realize that everybody can help to shape his or her community.

Personal Goals

You will learn a lot from your campaign volunteer work. You will understand more about the election process. You also may get ideas about what kind of career you want. Perhaps you will want to work as a public servant. If you are going to college, you may want to study political science. By working on a campaign, you also can get experience meeting people and working with them.

DESIGNING YOUR CAMPAIGN PROJECT

You can help a candidate's campaign in many ways. What you can do depends on your skills and goals. You might write articles for local or school papers or write letters to newspaper editors. You might hand out literature at busy shopping centers. You could hold up signs at intersections for passing drivers to see, or help set up speeches and rallies. You could stuff envelopes for mass mailings, put voters' names into a computer database for a mailing list, or answer phones in the campaign headquarters. Even routine office work can be fun in a high-energy, fast-paced campaign. Talk to the campaign manager or volunteer coordinator about what kind of help they need.

FAST FACT

General elections for president of the United States are every four years, on the first Tuesday after the first Monday in November.

Write up a plan for your campaign project. Make sure that it meets your personal goals. The plan should include:

- what kind of tasks you will perform
- the hours when you will work
- the training or supervision you will need

*Get involved and have a say
in choosing your government leaders.*

- how often you will need transportation
- what you hope to learn
- how you will report on your service-learning work at the campaign's end

Copies of the plan should go to your parents, your service-learning sponsor, and the campaign coordinator with whom you will be working.

THE RACE FOR MAYOR

Students from Central Park East High School in New York City volunteered on a candidate's campaign for mayor as a service-learning project. This team worked with the campaign manager at the candidate's headquarters. They helped to organize voter lists. They also answered phones and composed a mailing for a fund-raiser. The candidate invited them to a fund-raising event. At the event, they soaked up even more of the exciting campaign atmosphere.

Some of the students set up a meeting at school to share what they had learned. Others wrote a report on the voting process. They described what was good and bad about the process. Another group wrote about how the campaign worked. Together, they reflected on their experience and judged the value of their work. Their candidate lost, but the students still felt they had achieved several of their goals. They contributed to

A mayoral race can be a good opportunity to arrange for candidates to meet with voters.

Hearing a candidate speak will help you know which issues he or she feels are important.

democratic participation. They discovered a lot about issues and elections. And they learned how to be active citizens.

CANDIDATES NIGHT

Some schools do not allow student groups to work on individual campaigns. You still can work on an election. You can organize a meeting for citizens to meet all of the candidates.

Juniors at Orono High School in Maine are required to do a 30-hour service-learning project. A student named Russ organized a Candidates Night. He wrote a plan that explained how his community would benefit from the event. He also researched and wrote a paper on his project for his U.S. history class.

To organize the Candidates Night, Russell did the following:

- called all candidates for town council and the school committee and invited them to speak
- advertised the event in the local newspaper, on the local television station, and on the town's message center
- made sure each candidate knew the format, how long he or she would have to speak, and how long a time he or she had to answer questions from the audience
- directed the event
- got other students to help set up, welcome the audience, keep time during speeches, and take photographs

Russ kept a journal in which he described the frustrations and satisfactions of the project. When he needed advice, he went to his service-learning counselor. His counselor was a former town-council member.

Each spring, Orono High School holds a Service-Learning Exhibit Night. Each junior sets up a display about his or her project and gives an oral presentation. Russ was very pleased to describe the work he had done.

FAST FACT

United States senators serve six-year terms. U.S. representatives are elected every two years.

"This project has really helped me understand the election process," Russ said. "I'm planning to major in political science in college. I think organizing this service-learning project definitely enhanced my education."

Service-learning work can give you experience that can be helpful when you enter the real world.

ballot list of candidates for voting purposes

biased favoring one candidate

candidate person running for public office

editorial statement of opinion

federal referring to the government of the United States, based in Washington, D.C.

grassroots started by people in society, not by a central or higher authority

issues ideas or problems in society on which people take different or opposing positions

moderate to run a debate or issues forum

nonpartisan not favoring a particular political party or candidate

political party a group of officials, candidates, and voters who have similar ideas about government

representative democracy form of government in which voters elect officials to represent them

Berkowitz, Lois. *Active Citizenship Today Field Guide.* Washington, D.C.: Close Up Foundation, 1995.

Erlbach, Arlene. *The Kids' Volunteering Book.* Minneapolis, MN: The Lerner Publishing Group, 1998.

Lewis, Barbara A. and Pamela Espeland. *The Kids' Guide to Service Projects: Over 500 Service Ideas for Young People Who Want to Make a Difference.* Minneapolis, MN: Free Spirit Publishing, 1995.

Sobel, Syl and Pam Tanzey. *How the Government Works: . . . and How It All Comes Together to Make a Nation.* Hauppauge, NY: Barron's Educational Series, Incorporated, 1999.

Steins, Richard. *Our Elections.* Brookfield, CT: Millbrook Press, Incorporated, 1996.

ORGANIZATIONS

Close Up Foundation
44 Canal Center Plaza
Alexandria, VA 22314-1592
(800) CLOSE UP
Web site: *www.closeup.org*

Corporation for National Service
1201 New York Avenue, NW
Washington, D.C. 20525
(202) 606-5000
Web site: *www.cns.com*

The League of Women Voters
1730 M Street NW, Suite 1000
Washington, D.C. 20036-4508
(202) 429-1965
Web site: *www.lwv.org*

National Service-Learning Clearinghouse
University of Minnesota
1954 Buford Avenue
R-460 VoTech Building
St. Paul, MN 55108-6197
(800) 808-7378
Web site: *http://nicsl.jaws.umn.edu*

WEB SITES
Policy.com
www.policy.com
Policy.com is a policy news and information service full of activities, articles and analysis of issues and elections. Use its issues library, reach your representatives, find election dates, vote in its opinion polls, and much more.

Project Vote Smart

www.vote-smart.org

Project Vote Smart tracks the performance of the president, governors, Congress and state legislators. Enter your zip code to find your representatives and candidates. Go to their Youth Inclusion Program Web page for youth surveys, political games, and to do research on your representatives.

Selectsmart.com

www.selectsmart.com

Are you undecided? Match yourself up with a candidate or political party through this site's fun, interesting quizzes. Then follow through to find the candidates' policy positions and the parties' platforms. Selectsmart has lots of links to other political sites, too.

INDEX

INDEX

ABOUT THE AUTHOR
Sheila Klee is an editor and a writer in New York City. As a teen, she found political campaigning exciting and rewarding.